Contents

Movement and Feeding

Weird and wonderful animal eating habits

When we have lunch, we eat food that we've bought from a shop. But what do animals do? Here are some of the ways that animals get their food.

Leafcutter ants

Leafcutter ants cut leaves from trees and pile them up in their nests. These piles work like a compost heap and make a great place for fungus to grow.

leafcutter ants

The ants use the fungus to feed their larvae.

a red squirrel

Red squirrels

What do red squirrels do if they run out of food in the winter? They bite into the side of a maple tree and wait for the sweet sap to drip out. When the syrup dries, the squirrels eat it.

Giant anteaters

Anteaters use their large claws to break open ant hills. Then they poke in their long snouts and sweep up hundreds of ants with their super long tongues!

Things to do

Find out about an animal that has an unusual diet. Draw a picture of it and write about it.

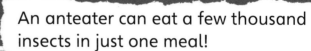
An anteater can eat a few thousand insects in just one meal!

Graph it!

Look at the table and graph and then answer the questions that follow on page 6.

Length of hand	Number of sweets grabbed
9 cm	10
9 1/2 cm	12
10 cm	13
8 1/2 cm	9
11 cm	13
10 1/2 cm	12
11 cm	14
12 cm	15
8 cm	10
13 cm	15
13 1/2 cm	16
12 1/2 cm	14

Graph to show a sweetie grab

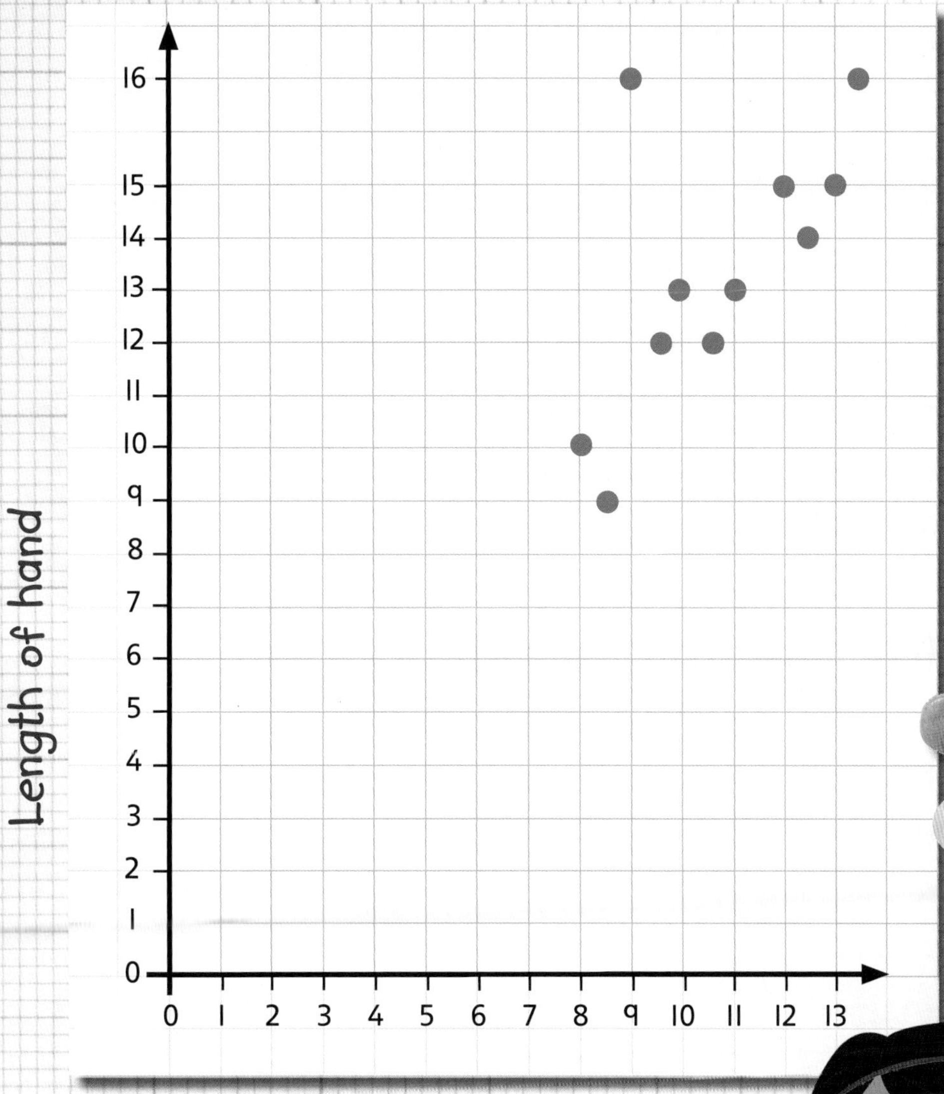

Length of hand

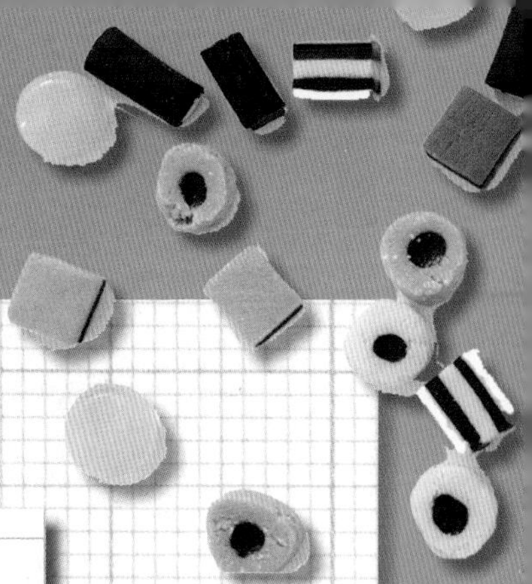

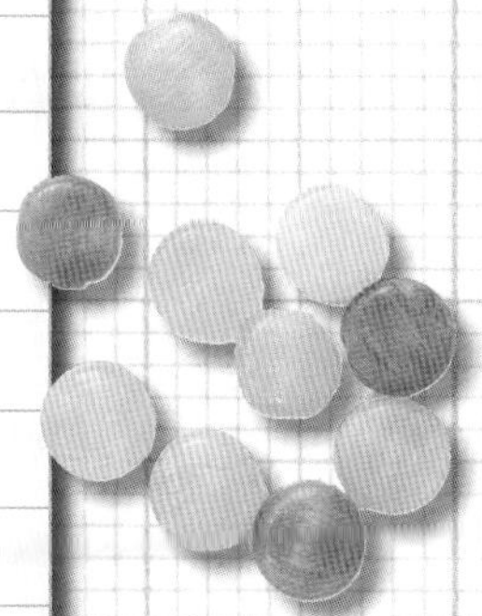

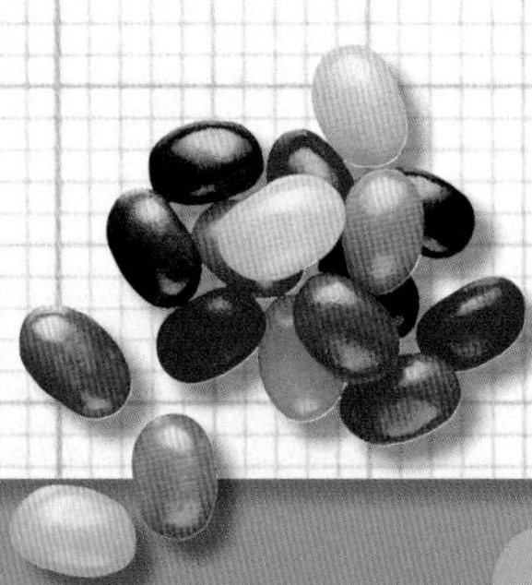

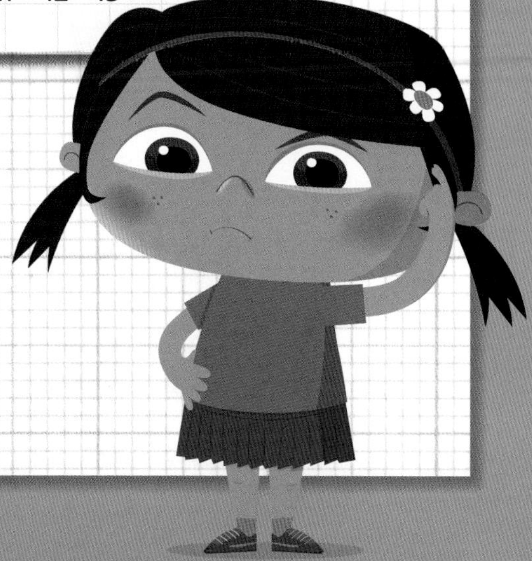

Interpret it!

Can you spot the five mistakes on the graph?

Use the table and graph to answer these questions.

1. Which hand grabbed the most sweets?

2. Which hand grabbed the least sweets?

3. How many more sweets were grabbed by the hand grabbing the most sweets than the least sweets?

4. Were any of the number of sweets grabbed by different size hands a surprise? Which ones?

5. Can you spot a pattern between the size of a child's hand and the number of sweets grabbed?

Things to do

Make up a question that the graph answers. Test your question on a friend.

Light and Shadows

Things to do

Name the sources of light and the reflectors in this picture. What would you see if it were night time in the picture?

Playing with shadows

Light travels in straight lines. It cannot go around corners. When light hits an object it is blocked and the object casts a shadow.

Try making an animal shadow using your hands.

Shadow puppets cast a shadow on a screen. The light is behind the screen. Where would you need to put the puppet?

Things to do

Find out about silhouette pictures from the 1700s. Try making your own pictures. Cut out your design on black paper and mount it on white paper.

Opaque, transparent and translucent

Light cannot pass through opaque materials. The shadow cast is strong and sharp.

Transparent objects let nearly all light through. They cast almost no shadow.

Some objects are translucent. They let some light pass through, but some light is scattered. The shadows they cast are weak and blurry.

Which of these bowls will cast the best shadow?

Make a silhouette gallery

You will need:

black
paper

strong light
source

chalk

scissors

1. Pin a piece of black paper onto a wall.

2. Place a friend, looking to the side, between the paper and a strong light source.

3. Draw around the shadow of their head cast on the paper.

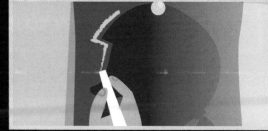

4. Cut out the shape and mount it in your gallery.

Can you guess who is who?

Sun safety

The Sun is our most powerful source of light. It is also very hot and can damage our eyes if we look directly at it. Our skin can burn if we spend too long in the Sun.

Things to do

What can we do to stay safe in the Sun? Make a list and compare it with your friend's list.

What Plants Need

Make a hydroponics vase

You will need:

- scissors
- large plastic bottle
- onion
- water

1 Cut the plastic bottle in half.

2 Turn the top half of the bottle upside down and put it inside the bottom half.

3 Trim the root off the onion and put it inside your container.

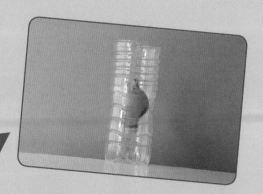

4 Fill the container with enough water to cover the bottom half of the onion.

5

Place the onion and container in a sunny place. Change the water every two days.

6

Observe and record any changes to the onion. Use photographs to record how the onion changes.

Scientists from NASA use hydroponics to investigate whether it might be possible to grow food on other planets.

Did you know?

Growing plants in watery solutions is called hydroponics. This comes from the Greek word *hydro* which means water.

Investigate it!

The school caretaker has been trying to find out how much grass seed she needs to repair the school field. This is what she did:

Test 1	
Test 2	
Test 3	
Test 4	

The caretaker gave one tray to each class. The children watered the seeds every day for two weeks.

After two weeks, the caretaker compared her test pot. Some trays of grass were growing better than others but she still did not know what she should do.

Things to do

Can you help the caretaker improve her investigation?

Soil

Soil contains nutrients that help plants grow. Plants need these nutrients to grow well. They do not need the other parts of the soil. Different plants need different nutrients. The nutrients in the soil can change how a plant looks.

Did you know?

You can change the colour of hydrangea flowers by adding different nutrients to the soil.

Blue hydrangeas grow in acidic soil.

You can turn a pink hydrangea blue by adding lemon peel to the soil!

Rocks and Soils

Rocks are everywhere

Do you know what is beneath your feet? Under a thin layer of soil there is a crust of rock which covers the whole surface of Earth.

Rocks don't all look the same. They have different colours and textures. Different rocks have different properties and we use them in different ways.

Look at how we use these rocks. Can you describe them? What makes them useful?

Things to do

Be a rock hunter! How many different things can you find made of rock?

Fabulous fossils

Some rocks are special. They contain fossils. Fossils are the remains of plants and animals that have been preserved in rock.

1

After their death, some animals were quickly covered by mud or sand.

2

As they decomposed, they were covered by more sediment (bits of rocks washed down by rivers).

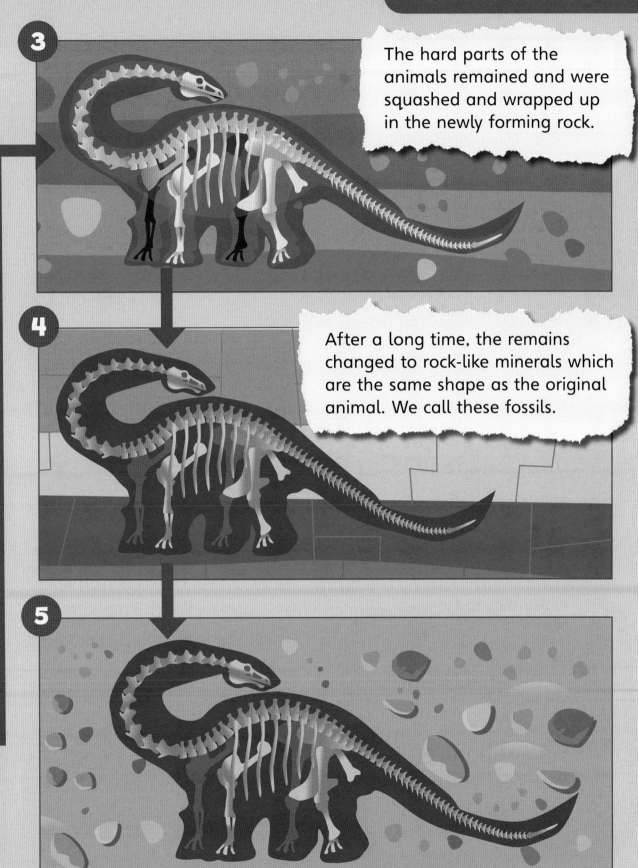

3

The hard parts of the animals remained and were squashed and wrapped up in the newly forming rock.

4

After a long time, the remains changed to rock-like minerals which are the same shape as the original animal. We call these fossils.

5

Fossil facts

Did you know?

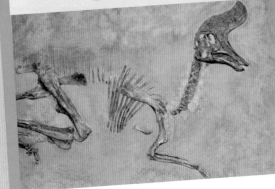

A fossil bone does not have any bone in it! It is more like a rock.

Did you know?

Some living things were preserved in amber. Amber is a hardened form of tree sap.

Did you know?

The word fossil comes from the Latin word *fossilis* which means 'dug up'.

Find out

Find out about Mary Anning, one of the very first fossil hunters. She discovered the first complete Ichthyosaurus when she was only 12 years old!

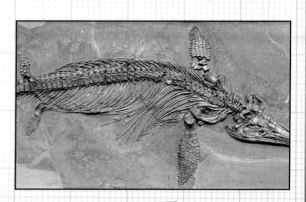

Soil is special

Soil is a mixture of tiny rock particles and pieces of plants. Worms in the soil help to break down the plants and keep the soil crumbly and full of air. Without soil and worms there would be no plants, grass or trees. Without these, there would be no us!

Land for farming needs fertile soil.

Old gravestones can be weathered like this.

Wearing down

Rocks are generally tough but over time, frost, wind and rain wear away the surface. Gradually the rock is worn away.

Things to do

Look in your area for signs that rocks have been changed by the weather.

Parts of Plants

Parts of plants

Lots of plants have the same parts but they may look very different.
Look at these plants. Can you identify the different parts?

water lily

lettuce

bramble

Banyan tree on a temple in Cambodia

Did you know?

The largest flower in the world is the titan arum, which can grow up to three metres tall. That's almost as big as an elephant!

Fabulous photosynthesis

Plants are amazing! They are the only living things that can make their own food.

Imagine you had some air containing carbon dioxide gas and some water. Now, just using those two ingredients, you have to make oxygen and sugars. How do you think you'd do that?

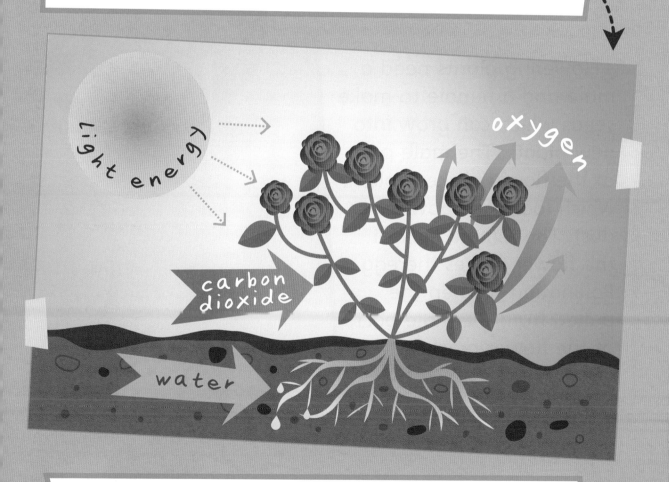

With a bit of sunlight to help, plants do just that. This process happens in their leaves and is called photosynthesis.

Perfect pollination

Pollination is part of the life cycle of flowering plants. Insects like bees and wasps, birds, animals and the wind carry pollen between flowering plants.

The pollinated flower turns into the apple fruit.

Flowering plants need a male and a female to make seeds which can grow into new plants. The male part of the flower makes pollen, which looks like powder or dust. The female part of the flower makes the egg. Pollination is when the pollen from the male part of the flower reaches the female part of the flower.

In the spring bees pollinate the flowers. The pollen rubs off onto their bodies as they collect nectar from the flowers.

Once pollen has moved between flowers, the plant becomes fertilised and makes seeds. Seeds can then become new plants.

The apple fruit contains the seeds.

The seeds take root in the ground and a new apple tree grows.

spring summer

Make a terrarium

A terrarium is a closed environment where you can see how a plant can use and recycle water.

You will need:
- large plastic bottle
- compost
- small stones or pebbles
- scissors
- small plants
- water

Assemble your terrarium like this:

Did you know?

A man in Surrey has kept plants growing in a terrarium for 53 years!

Magnets and Forces

Forces

You use forces every day to play and to make things move.

Which forces are being used in this picture?

Things to do

Can you think of another activity that uses forces to make things move?

Science Skills

Measure it!

Look at the picture. Decide how this car catapult works.

Some children decided to pull back the elastic band different amounts to see how far the car went.

What do you think of their ideas?

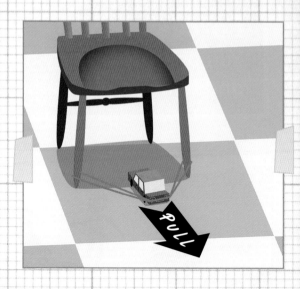

Let's do a small pull and a big pull on the elastic band.

Let's use 1 cm cubes to see how far back we pull the elastic band.

I think we should use a 30 cm ruler to measure the pull back.

The children also wanted to know how far the car moved forwards.

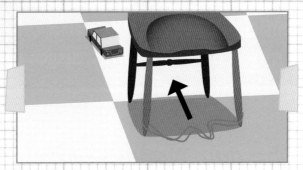

I think we should make a mark on the floor to show how far each car travels.

I think we should use a meter ruler to measure how far the car travels.

I think we should use a tape measure because it might go further than a metre.

Things to do

Make your own car catapult and measure how far the car travels when you change the pull on the elastic band.

A magnetic discovery

This ancient Greek legend tells the story of how a man called Magnes discovered magnets.

One day, Magnes was moving his sheep. His boots began to feel heavier and heavier. He stopped to see what was happening. Magnes found rocks which seemed to 'stick' to the iron nails in his boots.

Magnes told people about his discovery and they began collecting the rocks for themselves. No one could think of a use for them but they liked to play with them.

People believed that the rocks were magical.

Many years later people used magnets to make compasses. Now we use magnets in all sorts of things, from televisions to trains.

Did you know?

People in Britain used to call magnets lodestones, which means lead stone. Travellers would use lodestones to identify North which stopped them from getting lost.

Lodestone

Index